Israel

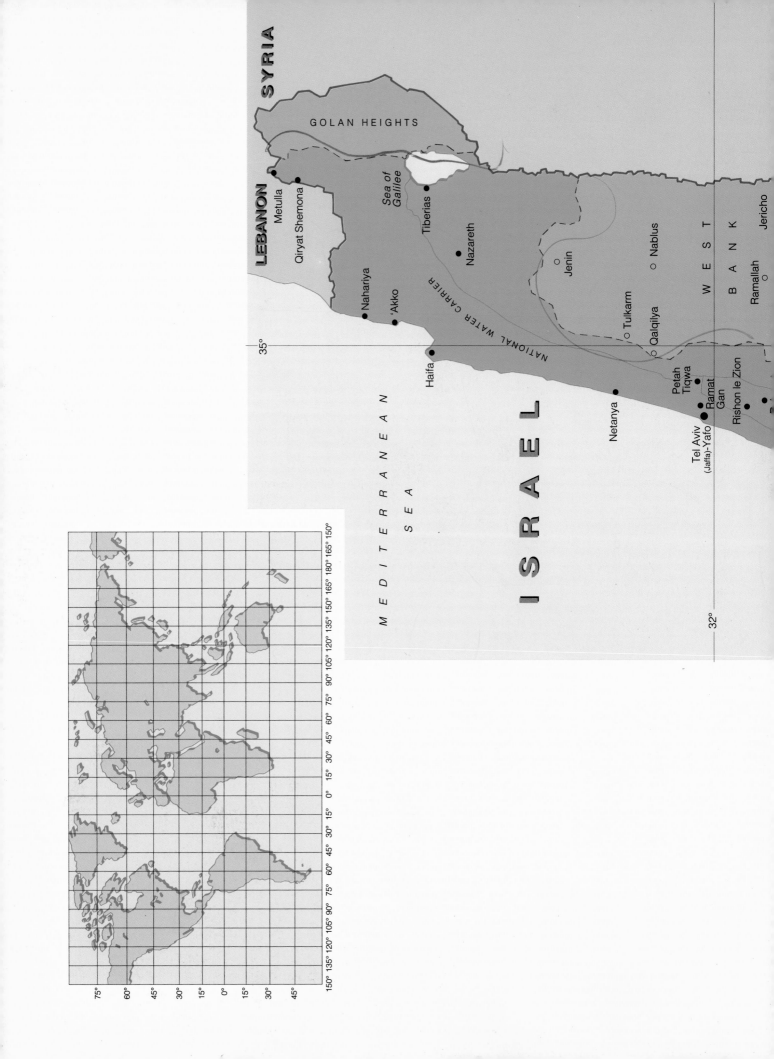

DISPUTED TERRITORIES

The three areas denoted by dotted lines
are disputed as follows:

GAZA STRIP – between Israel and Palestinians
GOLAN HEIGHTS – between Israel and Syria
WEST BANK – between Israel and Palestinians

Note: disputed territories are marked on this map,
but not on the smaller maps within the book

PALESTINIAN NATIONAL AUTHORITY

○ denotes town controlled by Palestinian National
Authority since 1994 (Jericho) or 1995 (6 other
towns in West Bank)

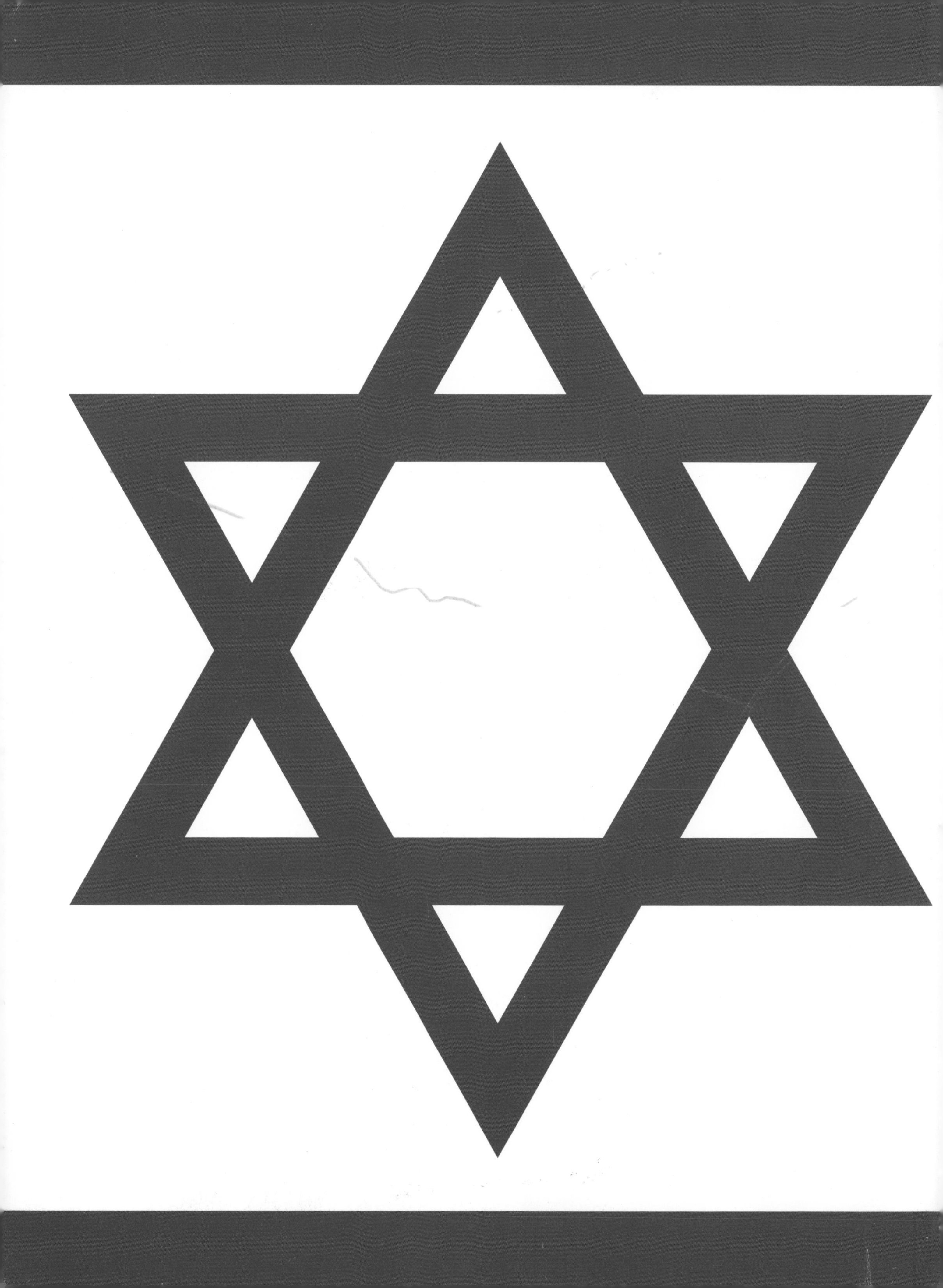

Israel

José Patterson

RSVP

RAINTREE STECK-VAUGHN
P U B L I S H E R S
The Steck-Vaughn Company

Published by Raintree Steck-Vaughn Publishers,
an imprint of Steck-Vaughn Company

Design and typesetting Roger Kohn Designs
Commissioning editor Debbie Fox
Editors Diana Russell, Pam Wells
Picture research Valerie Mulcahy
Illustration János Márffy

Special thanks to Melvin and Anita Cohen; the staff of the Public Affairs Department, Embassy of Israel; Shayla Walmsley of BIPAC (Britain Israel Public Affairs Centre); the library and office staff of the Oxford Centre for Hebrew and Jewish studies.

We are grateful to the following for permission to reproduce photographs:
Front Cover: Richard T Nowitz *above;*
ASAP (Rafael Macia) *below;*
ASAP Israel, pages 7 (Lev Borodulin), 25 (Rafi Magnes), 27 *right* (David Rubinger), 36 (Kenneth Fischer), 37 *above* (Michael Altschul), 38 (Lev Borodulin), 39 (Eiten Simanor); J Allan Cash, pages 14, 26; Stephanie Colasanti, pages 21, 28; Bruce Coleman, page 40 (Mark N Boulton); Colorific! page 29 (Sylvain Grandadam); Robert Harding Picture Library, pages 11 (E Simanor), 15 (ASAP/Israel Talby), 37 *below* (E Simanor); The Hutchison Library, pages 30 (Tony Souter), 34 (Robert Francis); Impact Photos, pages 8 (Christophe Bluntzer), 20 *above* (Mark Cator), 24 (John Cole); Katz Pictures, page 33 (Ricki Rosen/Saba/REA Israel, Ramat Gan 10/93 Magahori & Legziel Diamond Company); Magnum, pages 9 *above* (Fred Mayer), 10 *above* and *below* (Dennis Stock), 18 *above* (Micha Bar Am), 22 (Fred Mayer); Richard T Nowitz, page 19; Christine Osborne Pictures, pages 13 *below*, 18; Panos Pictures, page 27 *left* (Penny Tweedie); Rex Features, page 43 (Milner Moshe/Sipa Press); Tony Stone Images, pages 16/17 (Alan Smith); Sygma, page 20 *below* (L Gilbert); Topham Picturepoint, pages 23, 31, 42, (M Lipchitz); TRIP, pages 9 *below* (J Arnold), 32 (A Tovy); Weizmann Institute, page 35 (Miki Koren); Zefa Pictures, page 41.

The statistics given in this book are the most up to date available at the time of going to press

Printed in Hong Kong by Wing King Tong

1 2 3 4 5 6 7 8 9 0 HK 99 98 97 96

Library of Congress Cataloging-in-Publication Data
Patterson, José
Israel / José Patterson.
p. cm. — (Country fact files)
Includes bibliographical references and index
ISBN 0-8172-4627-4
1. Israel—Juvenile literature
I. Title. II. Series.
DS126.5.P338   1997
956.94—dc21   96-36975
CIP
AC

C O N T E N T S

Words that are explained in the glossary are printed in
SMALL CAPITALS the first time they are mentioned in the text.

⬚ INTRODUCTION

More than 3,000 years ago, Jewish people lived in the land of Israel in the Middle East. When the Romans conquered the area ten centuries later, the Jews were dispersed throughout the world. The land was later ruled by other peoples, such as Arabs and OTTOMAN TURKS.

The scattered Jewish communities suffered hatred and persecution in many countries. At the end of the 19th century, the ZIONIST movement was founded to help bring about their return to the same area of the Middle East, then called Palestine.

During World War II, six million Jews were killed in the Nazi HOLOCAUST. As a result, thousands of survivors joined other Jews in Palestine, and together they campaigned for the establishment of a national homeland. In 1947, the United Nations voted in favor of the division of Palestine into two states. Disagreement over this proposal led to the War of Independence in 1948, which was followed by the establishment of the State of Israel. Since then, Israel has found itself at war four more times (1956, 1967, 1973, 1982) with neighboring Arab countries who were opposed to the creation of the new state. In 1979, Egypt signed a peace treaty with Israel, and this was followed in 1994 by peace with Jordan. A comprehensive peace agreement for the region now seems to be more definite.

▼ *Jerusalem, the capital of Israel, is more than 3,000 years old. The Western Wall was once part of the ancient Jewish temple. Churches and mosques represent Christianity and Islam.*

In the half century since the state was founded, Israel has absorbed Jewish immigrants from all over the world. There are also significant Christian and Muslim minorities in the country, whose religious freedom is guaranteed by the state. Over the last 50 years, Israeli governments have built schools, hospitals, and good transportation links. They have also developed agriculture, industry, and tourism. In this book, you can find out about these successes and about the challenges that the country still faces.

ISRAEL AT A GLANCE

- Area: 8,495 sq mi (28,000 sq km)
- Population (1996): 5,685,000
- Population density: 669 people per sq mi
- Capital: Jerusalem, population 578,000 (1995)
- Other main cities (1995): Tel Aviv-Yafo 355,000; Haifa 246,000; Rishon le Zion 160,000; Petah Tiqwa 152,000
- Highest mountain: Hermon, 9,219 ft (2,814 m)
- Longest river: Jordan, 199 mi (320 km)
- Official languages: Hebrew and Arabic
- Major religions: Judaism, Islam, and Christianity
- Currency: Shekel, written as NIS
- Economy: Both agriculture and industry
- Major resources: Minerals from the Dead Sea
- Major products: Citrus fruits, high-tech equipment
- Major exports: Fruit, flowers, polished diamonds, electronic equipment, phosphates
- Environmental problems: Water shortage, increasing pollution, traffic density

▶ *A Hebrew fragment from the Dead Sea Scrolls, discovered in 1947 in the Qumran caves, where they had remained for 2,000 years.*

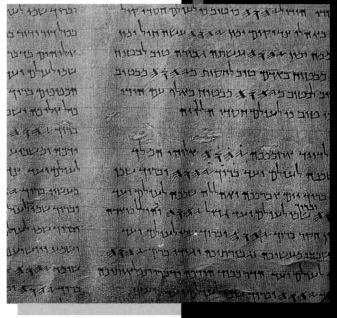

▼ *Tel Aviv-Yafo is the entertainment, business, and tourist center of Israel.*

THE LANDSCAPE

Israel is long and narrow, measuring only 293 miles (470 km) from north to south and up to 84 miles (135 km) east to west. It has land borders with Lebanon, Syria, Jordan, and Egypt. Israel has an amazing variety of landscape for such a tiny country. In the far north, the snowcapped Mount Hermon towers to a height of 9,219 feet (2,814 m). In stark contrast, the Dead Sea, at the southern end of the Jordan Valley, lies 1,312 feet (400 m) below sea level. It is the lowest point on earth.

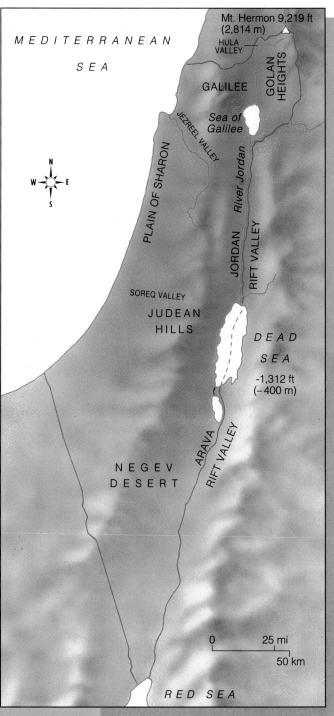

MEDITERRANEAN SEA

Mt. Hermon 9,219 ft (2,814 m)

HULA VALLEY

GALILEE

GOLAN HEIGHTS

Sea of Galilee

JEZREEL VALLEY

PLAIN OF SHARON

River Jordan

JORDAN RIFT VALLEY

SOREQ VALLEY

JUDEAN HILLS

DEAD SEA

-1,312 ft (–400 m)

NEGEV DESERT

ARAVA RIFT VALLEY

0   25 mi

50 km

RED SEA

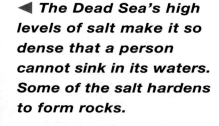

◀ *The Dead Sea's high levels of salt make it so dense that a person cannot sink in its waters. Some of the salt hardens to form rocks.*

There are four main geographical regions. The first is the coastal plain that runs parallel to the Mediterranean Sea. Fertile farmland borders the coast and extends up to 25 miles (40 km) inland. This is the most densely populated region in the country.

The Golan Heights make up the second region, originally formed by ancient volcanic eruptions. This area includes the limestone hills of Galilee, ranging from 1,640 to 3,937 feet (500 to 1,200 m) above sea level.

The third region is the Jordan Rift Valley

◀ *Mount Hermon straddles the borders of Israel, Lebanon, and Syria. The snow-capped mountain is excellent for winter skiing. In the foreground is Upper Galilee, where there is good farmland.*

KEY FACTS

● At 8,495 sq mi (22,000 sq km), Israel is about the same size as the state of New Jersey.

● A car trip from Metulla, the town farthest north in Israel, to Elat in the south can be completed in just 9 hours.

● At 696 feet (212 m) below sea level, the Sea of Galilee is the lowest freshwater lake in the world.

● The Dead Sea covers an area of 386 sq mi (1,000 sq km).

● The Negev takes up half of the country's land area, yet only 7% of the population live there.

and the Arava, part of the great Syrian-African Rift, which split the earth's crust millions of years ago. The Jordan River is fed by streams in the Mount Hermon area. It flows south through the Rift and the Hula Valley, descending over 2,297 feet (700 m) during its 186-mile (300-km) journey through the Sea of Galilee (also called Lake Kinneret or Lake Tiberias) before emptying into the Dead Sea.

The Negev is the fourth region. It is a huge triangle of land in the south of Israel. At its tip lies the Red Sea port of Elat. The landscape of the desert has sheer cliffs of colored sandstone, bare craggy peaks, vast craters, and dry riverbeds known as WADIS.

◀ *The Sea of Galilee is 13 miles (21 km) long and 7 miles (11 km) wide and lies between the hills of Galilee and the Golan Heights. In winter, strong winds blow through the narrow valley, whipping up stormy waves on the lake.*

Although it is a small country, Israel has a wide range of climate and weather, from temperate to tropical. This is because it straddles the continents of Africa and Asia. The main differences occur between the northern part of the country and the Negev in the south.

The north has a typical Mediterranean climate, with plenty of sunshine – long, hot, dry summers and mild, wet winters. Summer lasts from mid-April to October. In the coastal areas, the heat can be oppressive and humid, with temperatures rising to over 86°F (30°C). Welcome afternoon sea breezes help to moderate the heat.

Winter lasts from November to February. Rain can be very heavy at times, with almost three-quarters of the annual rainfall expected during the months of December, January, and February. Galilee is the wettest region, receiving over 39 inches (1,000 mm) of rain a year. But winters are generally mild, with plenty of intermittent sunshine. Frost and snow are very rare, except in the hill regions. In 1993, for example, Jerusalem had only two days of snow.

The amount of rain in the semidesert conditions of the Negev is very low, ranging from about 8 inches (200 mm) a year in the north to as little as 2 inches (50 mm) in Elat. From time to time, there are thunderstorms in this region. These result in flash floods, and every year people drown as wadis become

KEY FACTS

● Snow is rare outside the mountain regions. On the few days it snows in Jerusalem, excited schoolchildren, especially from the south, arrive by bus to make snowballs for the first time.
● In the rainy season, cloudbursts and violent storms can bring 4 in (100 mm) of rainfall in just 24 hours.

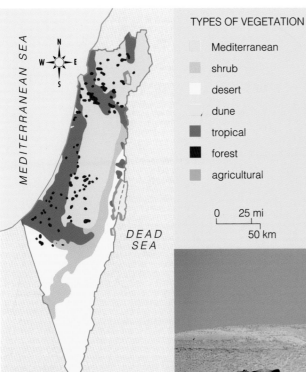

TYPES OF VEGETATION

Mediterranean

shrub

desert

dune

tropical

forest

agricultural

0   25 mi

50 km

flooded within minutes. By contrast, summer temperatures in the Negev soar to more than 93°F (34°C) in Beersheba and more than 104°F (40°C) in Elat.

The SHARAV (or Khamsin) is a scorching hot, dry desert wind, which blows from the Arabian Desert, south of Israel, from May to mid-June and from September to October. It lasts from two to five days at a time. Tiny particles of sand penetrate everywhere and make life very uncomfortable!

▶ BEDOUIN *in the Negev. Tents provide shade during the day and help keep out the cold at night.*

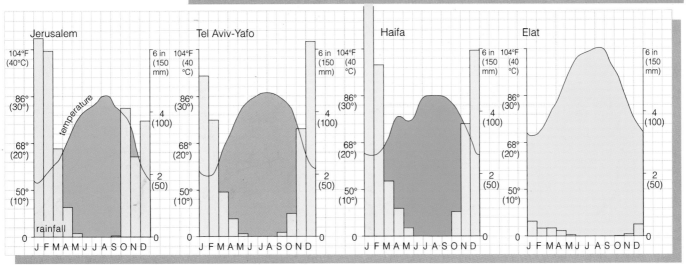

NATURAL RESOURCES

Israel has very few natural resources. It relies on imported fuel for its power plants. Oil is bought from countries such as Egypt, and coal is imported from South Africa.

Scientific research into the development of solar energy, using heat from the sun, has produced an important alternative source of energy. Per person, Israel is the world's largest user of domestic solar water heaters. By law, they are now installed in all new houses. A rooftop solar water heater requires about three hours of sunshine a

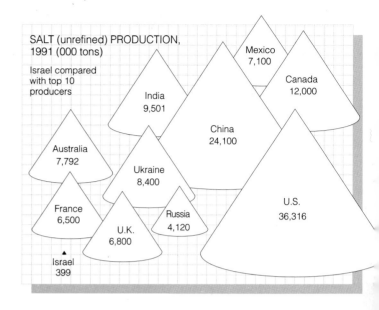

SALT (unrefined) PRODUCTION, 1991 (000 tons)

Israel compared with top 10 producers

Mexico 7,100

Canada 12,000

India 9,501

China 24,100

Australia 7,792

Ukraine 8,400

France 6,500

U.K. 6,800

Russia 4,120

U.S. 36,316

Israel 399

day to provide sufficient hot water for an average family of four. Even in winter, there is so much sunshine that an extra electric heater is needed only once in a while.

In 1989, an experimental power plant was set up in the Negev to produce electricity and steam using oil shale deposits — clay rocks that contain residues of crude oil. They are the most abundant fossil energy resource discovered in Israel. The oil shales can produce 5 megawatts of electricity and 50 tons of steam per hour, and may be used for both industrial and domestic purposes. Further development of these resources is being planned.

The country's most valuable natural resources are phosphates: potash, magnesium, bromine, and salt deposits from the Dead Sea. A significant amount is exported. These phosphates are valuable because of their use as chemical fertilizers.

Israel's only sources of fresh water are

◀ *Solar-powered street lights store energy from the sun to produce light at nighttime. They are especially useful at isolated bus stops.*

▶ *Fresh water is a precious resource. Some regions have a better supply than others. The National Water Carrier brings water from the north to the dry south, using aqueducts, tunnels, dams, canals, and pumping stations.*

KEY FACTS

● Between 1981 and 1995, Israel purchased 47 million tons of oil from Egypt for a total of about US$9 billion (at 1995 prices).

● Israel has a small copper mine near Elat, but high costs mean that it has been closed since the mid-1980s.

● Thousands of people from all over the world come to Israel to seek treatment for skin diseases and ailments such as arthritis, since it is believed that mud and sulfur from the Dead Sea may provide a cure.

the Jordan River, the Sea of Galilee, a few small rivers, and natural springs—all of which are located in the north. The heaviest rains also fall in the north. In 1964, the National Water Carrier was built to make the best use of these limited resources. It brings water, through a system of canals and giant pipelines, from the north to the semiarid regions in the south. This water is mainly used for irrigation and has helped to make parts of the desert fertile.

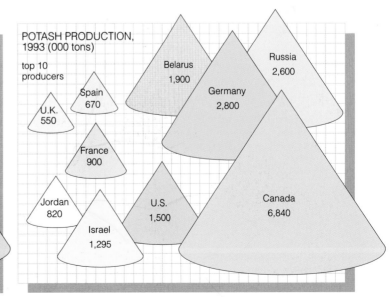

PHOSPHATE PRODUCTION, 1992 (000 tons)

top 10 producers

Germany 21,018
China 21,000
South Africa 3,080
Tunisia 6,400
Morocco 19,184
Brazil 2,459
Kazakhstan 6,680
U.S. 47,230
Jordan 4,296
Israel 3,596

POTASH PRODUCTION, 1993 (000 tons)

top 10 producers

Belarus 1,900
Russia 2,600
Spain 670
Germany 2,800
U.K. 550
France 900
Jordan 820
U.S. 1,500
Canada 6,840
Israel 1,295

POPULATION

Israel's fascinating multinational population is a melting pot of East and West. It includes both Jewish and non-Jewish citizens.

THE JEWISH POPULATION

When the state of Israel was founded in 1948, the Jewish population numbered 650,000. Today there are more than 4.6 million Jews, who have been drawn from almost every country in the world, with many differing cultures and religious customs. Nearly 5.7 million people today live in Israel, the majority of whom are native-born.

There are two main Jewish groups. ASHKENAZI Jews are of Central and Eastern European origin, while SEPHARDIC Jews come from North Africa, the Mediterranean area, and Arabic-speaking countries.

Israel has welcomed many different groups of Jewish people into the country. Following the end of World War II, refugees arrived from several European countries.

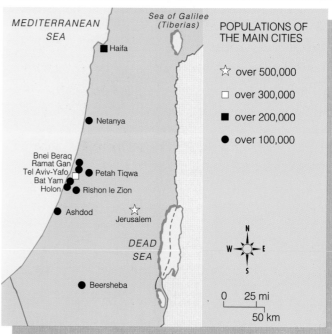

POPULATIONS OF THE MAIN CITIES

☆ over 500,000

☐ over 300,000

■ over 200,000

● over 100,000

MEDITERRANEAN SEA
Sea of Galilee (Tiberias)
Haifa
Netanya
Bnei Beraq
Ramat Gan
Tel Aviv-Yafo
Bat Yam
Holon
Petah Tiqwa
Rishon le Zion
Ashdod
Jerusalem
DEAD SEA
Beersheba

0 25 mi
50 km

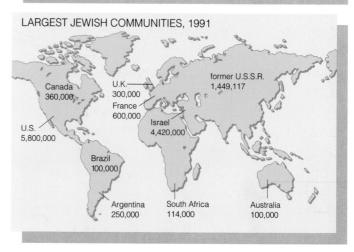

LARGEST JEWISH COMMUNITIES, 1991

Canada 360,000
U.K. 300,000
France 600,000
former U.S.S.R. 1,449,117
U.S. 5,800,000
Israel 4,420,000
Brazil 100,000
Argentina 250,000
South Africa 114,000
Australia 100,000

KEY FACTS

● Israel is a relatively young society. The average age is 26.6 years.
● In 1995, life expectancy was 76 years for men and 80 years for women—among the highest in the world.
● In 1995, the infant mortality rate was one of the lowest in the world—8.4 per 1,000 births.
● Hebrew and Arabic are the official languages. English is widely spoken. Many others are spoken as well, including Yiddish, Russian, and Amharic (Ethiopian).
● The Hebrew alphabet has 22 letters, plus 10 vowels that are written separately. Hebrew is written from right to left. "Shalom" means hello, goodbye, and peace.

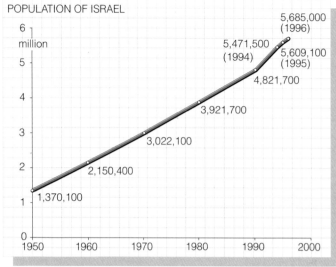

POPULATION OF ISREAL

- 1,370,100 (1950)
- 2,150,400 (1960)
- 3,022,100 (1970)
- 3,921,700 (1980)
- 4,821,700 (1990)
- 5,471,500 (1994)
- 5,609,100 (1995)
- 5,685,000 (1996)

▲ *In 1909, Tel Aviv was a tiny suburb of the ancient city of Yafo (Jaffa). Today, Yafo is part of the city area of Tel Aviv. The older buildings, with red-tiled roofs, are now part of a vast urban sprawl.*

The largest numbers came from Germany and Poland. After 1948, hundreds of thousands of Arabic-speaking Jews left their countries for Israel, too. They came from such places as Afghanistan, Algeria, Morocco, and Tunisia. Others came from as far away as Cochin in southern India. During the 1950s, almost the entire population of Jews from Yemen (as many as 42,000) were flown to Israel in what became known as "Operation Magic Carpet." The Yemenite Jews spoke Hebrew, which helped them to integrate successfully into the modern state. In the 1980s, 44,600 Jews from Ethiopia were brought to Israel to escape from civil war and religious persecution. Most recently, since the collapse of the Soviet Union in 1991, 627,000 Jews from the former Soviet Union have also settled in Israel.

Israel welcomes all newcomers and works hard to settle them. The Jewish Agency, with funds from international Jewish organizations and American grants and loans, has helped to provide immigrants with jobs, basic necessities, and a place to live.

ISRAEL'S NON-JEWISH CITIZENS

Israel has more than one million non-Jewish citizens—mainly Christian and Muslim Arabs and the DRUZE. The vast majority of the 835,000 Muslim Arabs are members of the Sunni sect and make up 76 percent (%) of the Arab population. They live in small towns and villages, mainly in the north of the country, with their own distinct culture and customs. There are also about 166,000 Christian Arabs, who belong to different religious groups. Most live in Nazareth, Haifa, and Jerusalem.

Nearly 10% of the Muslim Arab population are Bedouin. They belong to about 30 different tribes in the southern Negev and Galilee. Today, the Bedouin are no longer entirely nomadic. They live in permanent settlements where jobs are more readily available and their children can receive an education. But about 40% still follow their traditional desert way of life, traveling by camel in search of grazing land for their

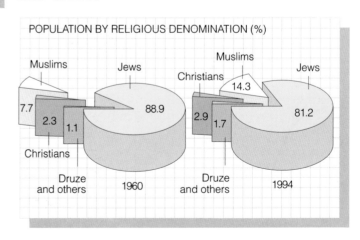

▲ *Greek Orthodox priests represent one of Israel's many Christian sects. The Orthodox calendar is different from that used by Catholics and Protestants. Christmas is celebrated on January 7.*

◄ *A street sign in Hebrew, Arabic, and English. Jerusalem's Armenian craft workers are famous for producing tiles like these.*

flocks of sheep and goats. They live in black goat-skin tents, which can be easily folded and transported on the backs of their camels.

THE CITIES

Many new development towns such as Dimona, Yeroham, and Qiryat Shemona were built in the 1950s to accommodate the growing population. Cheap apartment

POPULATION BY RELIGIOUS DENOMINATION (%)

Muslims Jews

Muslims

Christians

7.7 88.9

2.3 1.1

Christians

Druze and others 1960

Christians 14.3

Jews

2.9 1.7 81.2

Druze and others 1994

buildings were built as an emergency stop-gap measure to house Jewish immigrants, but many became overcrowded slums. Today, "Project Renewal" provides funds and volunteers, both Jewish and non-Jewish, from Europe and the U.S. to work in slum areas. They help to improve living conditions and to set up neighborhood committees and community centers.

More than 90% of Israelis today live in cities. Many modern urban centers are built on ancient sites mentioned in the Bible, such as Jerusalem, Tiberias, and Nazareth. Others began as agricultural villages and gradually grew into towns and cities. Because land is scarce, most city-dwellers live in apartment buildings. These normally have tiled floors and balconies. Modern garden apartments and co-ops are more numerous in suburbs and resort towns.

▼ *Passover is an important family holiday. In Israel, it lasts for 7 days (although Jewish people abroad may celebrate for 8 days). It begins with readings from the* HAGGADAH, *which describe how the ancient Israelites passed from slavery in Egypt into freedom. Special foods, like* MATZAH, *are eaten during this festival.*

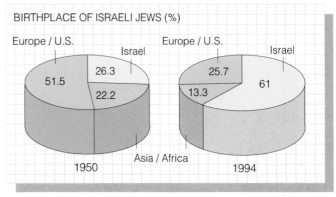

BIRTHPLACE OF ISRAELI JEWS (%)

1950: Europe / U.S. 51.5 | Israel 26.3 | 22.2 Asia / Africa

1994: Europe / U.S. 25.7 | Israel 61 | 13.3 Asia / Africa

RURAL LIFE

About 10% of the population live in rural areas. Approximately 2.4% are members of the country's 270 KIBBUTZIM. A kibbutz is a COOPERATIVE community, mainly agricultural, whose members share ideals, work, and responsibilities. They vote on important issues at regular meetings. Instead of wages, members receive a cash allowance, housing, food, clothing, and medical care. Families can eat at home or in the communal dining hall. Children are cared for and educated collectively, or in a group, so that their parents are free to work.

The MOSHAV is a collectively owned agricultural village. Unlike the kibbutz, its members live independent lives. Their produce is farmed and sold cooperatively. Israel has 450 moshavim, whose members make up 3.3% of the country's population.

▲ *Since 1984, more than 44,000 Jews from Ethiopia have settled in Israel. These Ethiopian children go to school in Jerusalem.*

▶ *Arabs, like Jews, are family-minded. No meal is complete without friends and relations to share specially prepared dishes.*

DAILY LIFE

◀ *The kibbutz is a mainly agricultural community where people share all work and responsibilities. It runs its own schools and kindergartens. These nursery school teachers are using large carts to take infants on their daily outing.*

WORK AND FAMILY LIFE

Israelis are hardworking people. Most work for five and a half days a week, although there is a growing trend toward a five-day week. People in offices work an eight-hour day, without a break, from 7:30 A.M. to 3:30 P.M. Banks, offices, schools, and Jewish stores close at noon on Friday and reopen on Sunday morning. This is because the Jewish Sabbath begins at sunset on Friday and ends on Saturday evening. There is no public transportation on Saturdays, except in Haifa, which has a large Arab population. Muslim stores are closed on Fridays and Christian stores on Sundays.

On Friday evenings, Jewish families and friends get together to enjoy the Sabbath meal. Before the Sabbath begins, religious Jews pray at the synagogue or at the Western Wall (the remains of the ancient temple in Jerusalem). Non-religious people may enjoy sports and leisure activities instead.

Family celebrations are important. They include BAR MITZVAHS and BAT MITZVAHS, too.

Israeli Arabs, both Christian and Muslim, live in traditional extended families, often with two or three generations gathered under one roof. They have their own culture and customs. For example, a wedding is celebrated by holding a special party every day for several days before the real marriage ceremony.

RELIGION

Religious freedom is granted to the entire population. Each religion has the right to practice its faith and appoint its own leaders. Jerusalem is the center of three great religions: Judaism, Christianity, and Islam. Their most sacred holy places in Jerusalem are near each other within the old walled city and are protected by law.

ORTHODOX (religious) Jews pray at the Western Wall. Nearby is the Dome of the

Rock with its magnificent gold dome. It is a monument to the Prophet Muhammad. On Fridays, their holy day, thousands of Muslims worship at the El Aqsa Mosque. Christians pray at the Church of the Holy Sepulchre, which contains the tomb of Jesus.

HEALTH

The National Health Service is based on medical services provided by insurance plans. Jerusalem's Hadassah Hospital is the largest in the Middle East. It treats more than 60,000 patients a year, regardless of religion or nationality.

Israel's emergency service, "Magen David Adom," provides ambulances, first-aid stations, and a blood-donor program. Around 4,500 volunteers are involved in the various branches.

There are also approximately 900 mother and child health centers in Israel that are run by local or national authorities.

MAJOR HOLIDAYS
Both the Jewish and Muslim calendars are based on the moon, not the sun, so dates of holidays vary each year.
In 1997, the major holidays are:

JEWISH HOLIDAYS

March 23, 1997	PURIM (commemorates the story of Queen Esther)
April 22–29, 1997	PASSOVER (commemorates the exodus of the Israelites from Egypt)
June 11, 1997	SHAVUOT (commemorates the giving of the Law to Moses)
October 2–3, 1997	ROSH HASHANAH (New Year 5758)
October 11, 1997	YOM KIPPUR (Day of Atonement)
October 26, 1997	SUKKOT (Feast of the Tabernacles)
December 24–31, 1997	HANUKKAH (Festival of Lights)

NATIONAL HOLIDAYS

May 4, 1997	Holocaust Martyrs' and Heroes' Remembrance Day
May 11, 1997	Remembrance Day for the Fallen of Israel's Wars
May 12, 1997	Independence Day
June 4, 1997	Jerusalem Day

MUSLIM HOLIDAYS

February 9–12, 1997	ID-UL-FITR (the end of Ramadan)
April 9–22, 1997	ID-UL-ADHA (related to the Haj, or pilgrimage to Mecca)
May 9, 1997	1 MUHARRAM (New Year 1418)
July 18, 1997	PROPHET MUHAMMAD'S BIRTHDAY

CHRISTIAN HOLIDAYS

March 31, 1997	EASTER SUNDAY (Catholic and Protestant)
April 27, 1997	EASTER SUNDAY (Orthodox)
December 25, 1997	CHRISTMAS DAY (Catholic and Protestant)
January 7, 1998	CHRISTMAS DAY (Orthodox)

◀ *At the age of 13, a Jewish boy or girl celebrates the bar or bat mitzvah and, according to tradition, becomes an adult. During the ceremony, he or she reads a passage from the* TORAH *scroll (Jewish scripture). The bar-mitzvah boy here wears a prayer shawl and skull cap.*

▶ *There are almost 800,000 Muslim Arabs in Israel, most of whom are members of the Sunni sect. Muslims turn in the direction of Mecca, the holy city, to say their prayers. They do this five times every day. These Arabs are praying at the El Aqsa Mosque in Jerusalem.*

EDUCATION

Both religious and secular (nonreligious) education have a high priority in Israel. The country spends 6 percent (%) of its GROSS NATIONAL PRODUCT (GNP) on education, compared with 7.5% in the United States.

There are three different types of Jewish schools: 69% of children attend state schools, 21% attend state religious schools, and 10% attend independent religious schools.

State education, including kindergarten for five-year-olds, is compulsory up to 16 years of age and free between the ages of five and 18. Up to the age of 13 years, children go to school from 8 A.M. till 1 P.M. High-school pupils (age 14 years and older) stay till 2 P.M. Before this, almost all three- and four-year-olds have some kind of preschool education that is not free.

KEY FACTS

● Women make up 40% of the workforce, and 68% of these are mothers with children under the age of 15.

● Israel has 176 doctors for every 10,000 people, compared with 225 in the U.S.

● Preschool attendance is the highest in the world; 97% of 3- and 4-year-olds go to a nursery school or play group.

● 13 Hebrew newspapers and 11 foreign-language newspapers are printed daily. The *Jerusalem Post* is the only English daily newspaper.

● There are 2 television channels as well as cable television. Programs are broadcast in Hebrew, Arabic, and several other languages.

◀ *Israeli schoolchildren start first grade at six years old. They study, among other subjects, Jewish history, the Hebrew Bible, and foreign languages, including Arabic (although this is not compulsory). Local geography is very popular, and children often go on field trips with their teachers.*

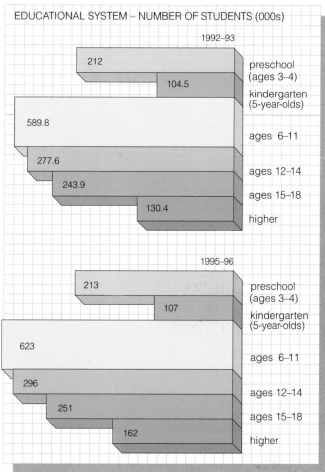

EDUCATIONAL SYSTEM – NUMBER OF STUDENTS (000s)

1992–93

212	preschool (ages 3–4)
104.5	kindergarten (5-year-olds)
589.8	ages 6–11
277.6	ages 12–14
243.9	ages 15–18
130.4	higher

1995–96

213	preschool (ages 3–4)
107	kindergarten (5-year-olds)
623	ages 6–11
296	ages 12–14
251	ages 15–18
162	higher

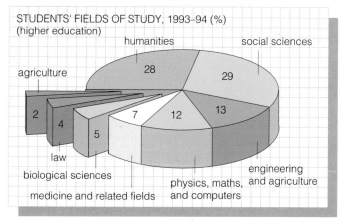

STUDENTS' FIELDS OF STUDY, 1993–94 (%)
(higher education)

- humanities 28
- social sciences 29
- agriculture 2
- law 4
- biological sciences 5
- medicine and related fields 7
- physics, maths, and computers 12
- engineering and agriculture 13

State religious schools emphasize Jewish studies and religious observance. Independent Torah schools are for ULTRA-ORTHODOX children. Boys and girls are taught in separate buildings.

Arab and Druze children go to Arabic-language schools, where they learn Hebrew as well as the history and culture of their own faiths. There are also a number of Jewish, Christian, and Muslim private schools.

Israel has eight universities, including the Open University of Israel, and a network of vocational training schools. About 35% of young people who are old enough to go to a university are students, compared with 58% in the U.S. and 20% in the U.K. But the average age of students is higher in Israel because of the need to do compulsory military service between 18 and 21. In the WEST BANK and Gaza, there are five teacher-training colleges and five universities.

The ULPAN system for adults and children provides free intensive language education programs for new immigrants. They are taught Hebrew, Jewish history, customs, and traditions.

SPORTS

League soccer and basketball are the most popular sports in Israel. Other sports include tennis, swimming, windsurfing, snorkeling, and scuba diving. Sports stadiums and training facilities are provided by regional and local authorities.

Jewish athletes from around the world compete in the Maccabiah Games, which are held in Israel every four years. The games are known as the "Jewish Olympics."

▼ *League basketball is organized at local, regional, and national levels. Matches always attract large, enthusiastic audiences.*

RULES AND LAWS

◀ *The menorah, a seven-branched candelabra, is the official emblem of the state of Israel. This menorah stands near the Knesset building in Jerusalem. Its carvings portray the history of the Jewish people.*

THE PRESIDENT
elected by the Knesset every 5 years

THE KNESSET
120 members
elected every
4 years

THE GOVERNMENT
(executive)

legislative

THE JUDICIARY

THE ATTORNEY-GENERAL

COURTS OF LAW

THE PRIME MINISTER

THE SPEAKER

LOCAL COUNCILS

MAYORS

MINISTRIES

COMMITTEES

STATE COMPTROLLER

COUNCIL HEADS

T H E   E L E C T O R A T E

Israel is a parliamentary democracy. The Knesset, or parliament, is elected every four years. It has 120 members, including Arab and Druze representatives. The head of state is the president, who is elected by members of the Knesset and serves for a period of five years.

Everyone over 18 has the right to vote. Voters choose both a candidate for prime minister and the political party they want to represent them. The prime minister is head of the government. There are two main parties, Labor and Likud (conservative). The Likud party was elected in 1996, but without a clear majority. It depends on the support of smaller, mainly religious, parties to maintain itself in power.

Military service in the Israel Defense Force (IDF), which includes the army, navy, and airforce, is compulsory for all eligible, medically fit men and women at the age of 18. Men serve for three years, and women for two. After this, men serve part-time in the Army Reserves until they reach 45 years of age and in the Civil Defense until they are 55 years old. Married women, ultra-Orthodox Jews (who devote their lives to religious studies), and non-Jews are exempt from military service.

Israel depends upon the IDF to protect its borders, since some of the country's Arab neighbors refuse to recognize its existence. Border clashes and terrorist attacks are common. After the war in 1967, Israel took over the Golan Heights area from Syria, and today there are still disputes about where the border between the two countries should lie.

In 1994, the Palestinian National Authority (PNA) was granted control in Gaza and Jericho. In 1995, it also gained control of parts of the West Bank where 70 percent (%) of the area's Arab population live, including six major towns. The PNA opposes any further Jewish settlements in these areas. The status of Hebron is still under negotiation.

A change of government in Israel in 1996 slowed down the peace process with the Arab countries. A major obstacle to peace in the region is that both Jewish and Muslim extremists continue to reject the idea of reaching an agreement.

▼ *Women soldiers serve in most branches of the Israel Defense Force but do not go into battle.*

KEY FACTS

● Israel's flag is based on the design of a Jewish prayer shawl with a blue Star of David.
● Although Arabs are exempted from the IDF, there are many Bedouin volunteers, who are famous for their tracking and scouting skills.
● The growth of Jewish Orthodox extremism in Jerusalem has led to violent clashes with secular Jews over the use of private vehicles on the Sabbath. Police have had to control the disturbances.

▲ *The IDF and the Palestine police force now have joint patrols in the West Bank and Gaza.*

✡ FOOD AND FARMING

Irrigation has revolutionized agriculture in Israel. Since 1948, the total area under cultivation has more than doubled to 1.1 million acres (440,000 ha), while irrigated land has increased eightfold to about 593,000 acres (240,000 ha). Israel's agricultural success has been achieved by close cooperation between farmers and agricultural scientists. The old, costly, and wasteful irrigation method of using water sprinklers has been replaced by a computerized drip system. Perforated plastic tubing allows each plant to be supplied with nutrients and water. This technique has turned thousands of acres of desert into arable land. In addition, new varieties of crops have been developed that can tolerate the desert climate and give improved yields. The kibbutz and moshav farming communities supply households with fruit, vegetables, dairy products, and poultry, in addition to trout, carp, and salmon, which are bred in fish farms.

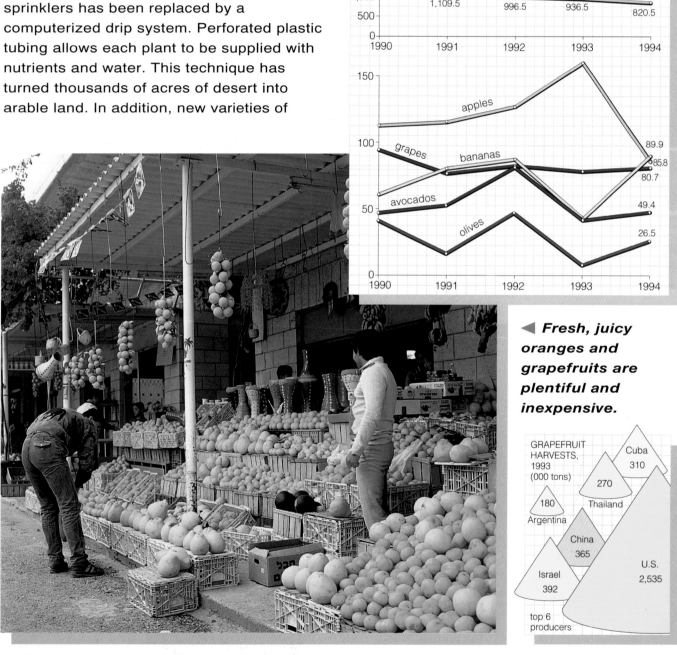

HARVESTS (000 tons)

citrus fruit: 1,506.1 (1990), 1,109.5 (1991), 996.5 (1992), 936.5 (1993), 820.5 (1994)

apples, grapes, bananas, avocados, olives: 89.9, 85.8, 80.7, 49.4, 26.5 (1994)

◀ **Fresh, juicy oranges and grapefruits are plentiful and inexpensive.**

GRAPEFRUIT HARVESTS, 1993 (000 tons)

Cuba 310
Thailand 270
Argentina 180
China 365
Israel 392
U.S. 2,535

top 6 producers

Farming practices are changing, but some Israeli Arab farmers still use traditional methods such as TERRACING hillsides. They grow grapes and olives on their small farms, and herd sheep for meat and wool.

Although pastureland for cows is scarce, milk production is high for a small country.

In 1993, the average dairy cow produced 2,613 gallons (9,500 kg) of milk. The most successful dairy producer was kibbutz Negba, where the average annual output was 3,257 gallons (11,845 kg).

Israel's chief agricultural imports are grain, oil seeds, meat, coffee, cocoa, and

◄ *Early-morning shoppers at this market stand like to buy their bread piping hot, straight from the ovens. Large, flat Iraqi bread is baked on the sides of the oven. Round bagels, often sprinkled with sesame or poppy seeds, are always favorites.*

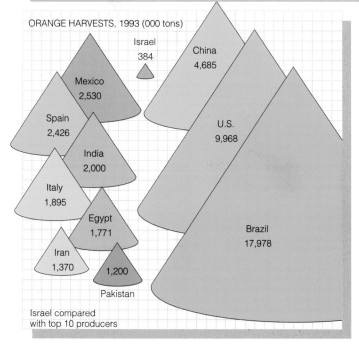

ORANGE HARVESTS, 1993 (000 tons)

Israel 384
China 4,685
Mexico 2,530
Spain 2,426
U.S. 9,968
India 2,000
Italy 1,895
Egypt 1,771
Iran 1,370
1,200
Brazil 17,978
Pakistan

Israel compared with top 10 producers

KEY FACTS

● Ancient Jewish laws require all fields to be tilled but not sown, every 7th year.
● Between 1985 and 1994, individual consumption of fresh vegetables rose by 32%, from 295 pounds (134 kg) to 390 pounds (177 kg) a year.
● The English language does not have an equivalent of the French saying "Bon appetit" (good appetite). The Israelis say "Be'tayavon," which means the same.
● Israelis have an addiction to chewing "garinim"—roasted and salted sunflower, pumpkin, and watermelon seeds. They are eaten, like potato chips, anywhere, anytime.

◄ **Falafel stands are part of the Israeli way of life. It is important not to overfill this pocket sandwich. Carried in a napkin, it can be eaten and enjoyed anywhere.**

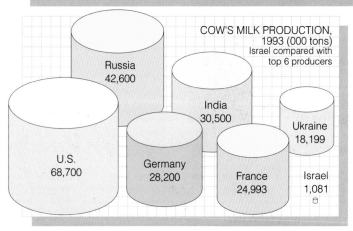

COW'S MILK PRODUCTION, 1993 (000 tons) Israel compared with top 6 producers

Russia 42,600
India 30,500
Ukraine 18,199
U.S. 68,700
Germany 28,200
France 24,993
Israel 1,081

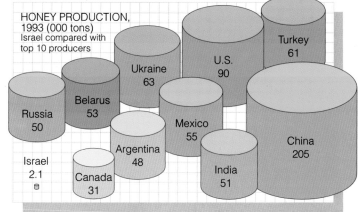

HONEY PRODUCTION, 1993 (000 tons) Israel compared with top 10 producers

Turkey 61
U.S. 90
Ukraine 63
Belarus 53
Russia 50
Mexico 55
China 205
Argentina 48
Israel 2.1
Canada 31
India 51

sugar. Its most successful agricultural exports include citrus fruits, melons, tomatoes, cucumbers, and avocados.

The unique blend of East and West in the country has produced a great variety of Jewish ethnic cooking traditions, ranging from small pastries filled with cheese, from the Middle East, to borscht (a thick beet soup, from Eastern Europe). Bread comes in every shape and size. Freshly baked braided CHALLAH breads are bought on Fridays for the Sabbath meal. Soft, flat Arab pita bread is well known. Its hollow "pocket" is filled with fried chickpeas, pickles, salad, and a spicy sauce. This is falafel, the country's most

famous snack food. There is an entire street of falafel stands in Tel Aviv.

Most Jewish restaurants and all official public eating places serve KOSHER food, prepared according to ancient Jewish dietary laws. These forbid the eating of certain foods, such as all products derived from pigs and shellfish. Meat and dairy foods may not be eaten together. Not all Israelis observe these rules. Muslims have their own dietary rules that also forbid the eating of pork and similar products.

Local produce and imported American and European foods line the shelves of modern air-conditioned supermarkets.

Domestic goods include many kinds of delicious yogurts and white cheeses made from sheep, goat, and cow's milk. Outdoor markets attract shoppers who like to browse among mountains of fruit and vegetables that are picked and delivered daily. There are also stands that specialize in roasted nuts and seeds, dried fruit, and a great range of aromatic herbs and spices. Street kiosks sell fresh orange, grapefruit, carrot, and kiwi juices, squeezed while you wait.

Every Jewish festival is celebrated with its own special food. Apples and honey are symbolic of a sweet New Year, while doughnuts and potato LATKES are eaten at Hanukkah and HAMANTASCHEN at Purim. During the seven days of Passover, ordinary bread and flour products are replaced by matzah and matzah meal. Matzabrie (fried matzah), coconut pyramid cakes, and kneidlach (soup dumplings) are all favorites.

Arab specialities include puff pastries called kunafa and sambusak. Kunafa has a sweet filling, while sambusak may be filled with either sweet or savory items.

▼ *The lakeside restaurant at kibbutz Ein Gev specializes in serving St. Peter's fish (also called "amnon") that is caught in the Sea of Galilee.*

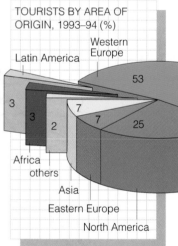

◀ *Israelis refer to Elat as "sof olam" —the end of the world! Thousands of tourists enjoy the year-round sunshine at this resort on the Red Sea. Outdoor activities include sailing, scuba diving, and snorkeling among rare tropical fish and corals.*

TOURISTS BY AREA OF ORIGIN, 1993–94 (%)

Western Europe 53
Latin America
North America 25
Eastern Europe 7
Asia 7
others 2
Africa 3
3

EXPORT MARKETS AND DEVELOPMENTS

During the first half of the 1990s, Israel's economy, with the help of aid from the U.S. and international Jewish organizations, had a high growth rate compared to those in the West. This economic achievement has attracted foreign investment to the value of US$1 billion.

Israel has a small economy and a limited domestic market. Economic growth depends on finding new export markets. In the past, the political situation prevented trade with most of Israel's neighbors. Since the start of the new round of peace talks, which began in 1994, trade agreements have been signed with Egypt, Jordan, Tunisia, and Morocco. In addition to Western markets, Israel also has good trade links with China, India, and South Korea. Japan has opened

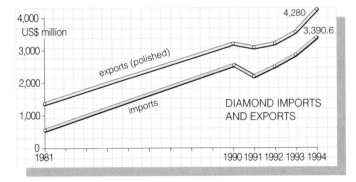

DIAMOND IMPORTS
AND EXPORTS

4,000 US$ million
3,000
2,000
1,000
0
1981 1990 1991 1992 1993 1994

exports (polished) 4,280
3,390.6
imports

DESTINATION OF
DIAMOND EXPORTS,
1994 (%)

Switzerland
U.S.
45
3 8
10 17 17
others
Belgium Japan
Hong Kong

► *Polished diamonds are a key export. Here, the stones are examined for imperfections. It takes great skill to cut them correctly.*

an official trade office in Tel Aviv, too.

Israel has a well-trained, highly skilled workforce but lacks most basic raw materials. Industry, therefore, concentrates on manufactured products and scientific and technological development. Israel allocates 10 percent (%) of its national spending to scientific research. Developments in agricultural techniques and technology, fine chemicals, computer hardware and software, and medical electronics have reached international standards. Israel has 90% of the world market in some areas of electro-optics, and the U.S. buys almost a third of its surgical lasers from Israel.

THE DIAMOND INDUSTRY

Israel is the world's leading exporter of polished diamonds. The industry was set up in the 1950s by a group of skilled Belgian and Dutch Jewish refugees. Exports now exceed US$4 billion a year. The Diamond

Exchange in Ramat Gan, near Tel Aviv, is the center of the industry. Not all diamonds are made into jewelry. Some of the rough, uncut stones, which are imported from Asia and Africa, are used in drilling and cutting machines.

TOURISM

Because of Israel's climate, tourists visit the country all year round. The tourist industry is worth about US$2 billion annually and plays a vital role in Israel's economy. More than 1.5 million tourists arrive every year. Vacationers flock to resort hotels. International and domestic flights take visitors directly to Elat for water sports and winter sunshine. Archaeological sites and excavations are another important attraction. Youth hostels are crowded with European backpackers, and many young people join kibbutz volunteer programs. Among the tourists are about 300,000 pilgrims who join tours of the Holy Land that are specially organized to include sacred Christian sites.

A large number of tourists are Jewish people from abroad. They visit relatives, take courses at a religious center or university, celebrate Jewish festivals, or visit Yad Vashem in Jerusalem, the official memorial to the six million Jews killed in the Nazi Holocaust of World War II.

CONSTRUCTION

In the first 25 years of the new state, residential building accounted for 84% of total construction. This percentage is continually fluctuating to meet the needs of the growing population and new

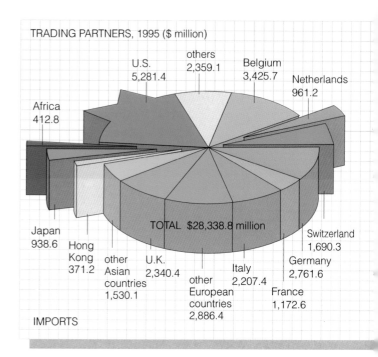

TRADING PARTNERS, 1995 ($ million)

U.S. 5,281.4
others 2,359.1
Belgium 3,425.7
Netherlands 961.2
Africa 412.8
TOTAL $28,338.8 million
Switzerland 1,690.3
Japan 938.6
Hong Kong 371.2
other Asian countries 1,530.1
U.K. 2,340.4
Italy 2,207.4
Germany 2,761.6
other European countries 2,886.4
France 1,172.6
IMPORTS

▼ *The Dead Sea Works company uses modern, computerized techniques to extract phosphates: potash, magnesium, bromine, and salt. Exports are worth US$500 million a year.*

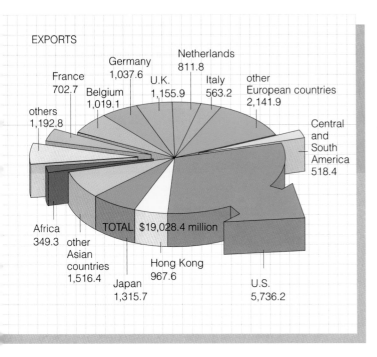

EXPORTS

France 702.7
Germany 1,037.6
Netherlands 811.8
Belgium 1,019.1
U.K. 1,155.9
Italy 563.2
other European countries 2,141.9
others 1,192.8
Central and South America 518.4
Africa 349.3
other Asian countries 1,516.4
Japan 1,315.7
Hong Kong 967.6
U.S. 5,736.2

TOTAL $19,028.4 million

▶ *The Weizmann Institute in Rehovot is an important science research center. Scientists help industry by developing a wide variety of electronic and high-tech equipment for export.*

KEY FACTS

● The Israeli workforce is divided as follows: 33% in industry, agriculture, and construction; 6% in transportation and communications; and 61% in public and commercial services.

● Polished diamonds from Israel account for 35% of those used in new jewelry throughout the world.

● On average, visitors spend 17.5 nights in Israel, putting the country in the top 5 tourist destinations measured by length of stay.

● Haifa Technion University, where farmers and scientists work together, has the largest agricultural engineering faculty in the world.

immigrants. A total of 83,000 new apartments were built in 1991, compared with 43,000 in 1992 and 33,600 in 1993.

HISTADRUT

The majority of Israel's labor force, including both Jews and Arabs, belong to the Histadrut—the General Federation of Labor. Its members come from all branches of the economy, from dock-workers to bank managers. The Histadrut provides jobs in addition to representing its members. Until recently, it operated Israel's largest health insurance program, and it continues to provide educational and welfare services for its members.

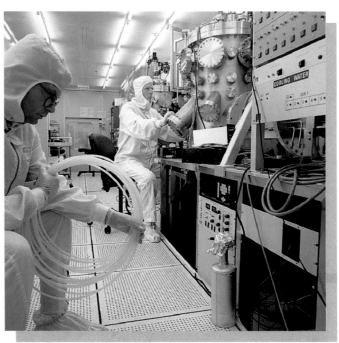

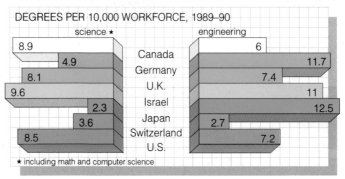

DEGREES PER 10,000 WORKFORCE, 1989–90

	science ★	engineering	
Canada	8.9	6	
Germany	4.9		11.7
U.K.	8.1	7.4	
Israel	9.6		11
Japan	2.3		12.5
Switzerland	3.6	2.7	
U.S.	8.5	7.2	

★ including math and computer science

TRANSPORTATION

Israel has a modernized road network system that links the country's major business, cultural, and vacation centers. Road signs are in Hebrew, English, and Arabic. Rising prosperity has enabled more people to buy cars. In 1994, there were more than 1,470,000 private cars on the roads, and Israel now has one of the most congested road systems in the world. There are about 500 fatal road accidents every year, and the death toll continues to rise. Experts believe that, in spite of vehicle inspections, they may be caused by a high percentage of inexperienced teenagers driving unsafe, secondhand cars, in

▼ *Bus stations are always crowded because the service is so popular. Some local buses run till midnight. Senior citizens can travel for half price.*

addition to too many motor scooters and motorcycles. A total of 58,323 motorcycles were purchased in 1994 alone.

One of the most popular means of transportation in Israel is traveling by bus. The Egged Bus Company is a cooperative owned by its drivers. It is the third largest bus company in the world in terms of passengers carried, with an income of US$342 million in 1991. It has a fleet of 4,000 air-conditioned buses that operate all urban and intercity services, except in Tel Aviv, where another company operates. Buses do not run between dusk on Friday and dusk on Saturday, except in Haifa.

The SHERUT TAXI is special to Israel. It is a shared taxi that holds up to seven passengers, operating a direct service between its own fixed stations. There is a set price, which is a little more than the

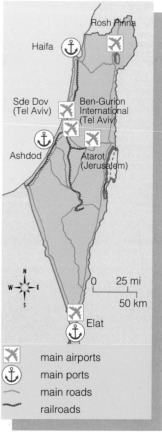

Rosh Pinna

Haifa ⚓ ✈

Sde Dov (Tel Aviv) ✈

Ben-Gurion International (Tel Aviv) ✈

Ashdod ⚓

Atarot (Jerusalem) ✈

N
W — E
S

0   25 mi

50 km

✈ Elat
⚓

✈   main airports
⚓   main ports
～   main roads
⌇   railroads

▲ *Tel Aviv's modern station caters to a growing number of railroad passengers. Two new commuter stations are used for travel between the city and the suburbs.*

bus fare for the same journey.

Israel's international airline is El Al. In 1993, its income was US$ 947.1 million. In the same year, it carried 2,154,000 passengers into and out of Israel. The company is also a major cargo carrier for Israel's agricultural and industrial exports.

Ben-Gurion International Airport in Tel Aviv handled 6.8 million passengers in 1995. This was 15 percent (%) more than the 1994 total. A modern terminal, which has improved passenger services, was opened in 1994. Arkia, Israel's domestic airline, links the major cities.

Railroad passenger services are limited and unprofitable. There are railroad links between Jerusalem, Tel Aviv, Haifa, and Nahariya. However, trains have recently become more of an accepted method of passenger travel. This is due to the

▼ *Good road links have brought benefits even to remote communities. But, in spite of six-lane highways serving the ports and industrial and business districts, traffic congestion has become a major problem.*

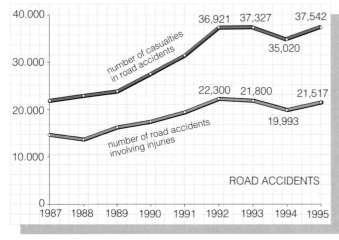

number of casualties in road accidents

| | 36,921 | 37,327 | 37,542 |
| | | 35,020 | |

number of road accidents involving injuries

| | 22,300 | 21,800 | 21,517 |
| | | 19,993 | |

ROAD ACCIDENTS

1987 1988 1989 1990 1991 1992 1993 1994 1995

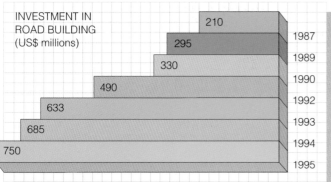

INVESTMENT IN ROAD BUILDING (US$ millions)

Amount	Year
210	1987
295	1989
330	1990
490	1992
633	1993
685	1994
750	1995

development of new commuter lines as a welcome alternative to road delays. A major new railroad expansion plan, "Project Railroad 2000," which will include Israel's first underground train, is being planned. Freight train services operate in the south, serving Ashdod and the mineral quarries near Dimona.

The modern deepwater ports of Haifa, Elat, and Ashdod serve international shipping. Haifa is one of the largest container ports in the Mediterranean, in addition to being a passenger terminal.

▼ **Haifa is a modern port used by luxury liners, tankers, and cargo boats. Here, oranges are being loaded for shipment to Europe.**

KEY FACTS

● In 1996, the government decided to take tough measures to reduce road accidents by increasing traffic fines. Failure to stop at traffic lights will cost a driver US$625 instead of US$125. A repeat offense will cost US$940 instead of US$170.

● In 1995, the U.S. had 19 vehicles per mile of road, Spain 25, Japan 32 and Germany 37. Israel had 100: the world's highest figure.

● Traffic laws are strict. Seat belts are compulsory. Speed limits are 56 mph (90 kph) on highways and 32–44 mph (50–70 kph) in urban areas.

● The journey from Tel Aviv to Jerusalem takes 1 hour, 40 minutes by train and costs US$4.20. The same journey by Sherut taxi takes 45 minutes and costs US$4.60.

THE ENVIRONMENT

◀ *Tree planting helps to prevent soil erosion and creates recreation areas. These children are planting saplings to celebrate Tu B'Shevat – Israel's Arbor Day. Millions of trees are planted every year in Israel.*

Planting trees to help protect the soil from erosion became a national priority after 1948. Since then, 200 million trees have been planted all over the country. Four million trees are planted every year. Tu B'Shevat, the 15th day of the Jewish month of Shevat, is Israel's Arbor Day. It is celebrated by planting trees, a practice often used to mark birthdays and special events.

Several nature conservation groups, appointed by the government, work closely together. For example, the Society for the Protection of Nature operates 24 field schools, providing intensive educational programs on nature protection and conservation.

More than 1,545 square miles (4,000 sq km) of land have been set aside for Israel's 280 nature preserves. The Hula lake area was once malarial swamp and marshland. Between 1951 and 1957, a massive

drainage project was begun here to create new farming land, but 766 acres (310 ha) were left untouched. In 1964, this area was officially declared Israel's first wildlife nature preserve.

Because Israel lies at the crossroads of three continents, plant and animal life is especially rich. Creatures such as the ibex, leopard, and vulture are protected species. The country has more than 2,800 different types of plants and about 380 different species of birds. Every year, hundreds of thousands of migrating birds pass through Israel. Places like the Hula preserve provide magnificent opportunities for serious bird-watching.

Hai-Bar, which means "wildlife," was established in the mid-1960s to reintroduce animals that once lived in Israel. So far the white oryx, Asiatic wild ass, addax antelope, and a local species of ostrich have been rescued from near extinction and

▲ *The ibex lives in the mountainous regions of the Negev. In spite of its great size and heavy horns, it is surprisingly nimble and sure-footed.*

successfully reintroduced into the wild. Similarly, Neot Kedumim is a botanical preserve that collects and conserves plants mentioned in the Bible.

Pollution in Israel comes from highly industrialized urban areas, 70 percent (%) of which are concentrated along the narrow Mediterranean coastal strip. Israel belongs to the Mediterranean Action Plan —

MEDITERRANEAN SEA

Nahal Ayoun

Tel Dan

Nahal Hermon

En Afiq

Hula

Gamla

Nahal Mearot

Soreq Cave

En Gedi

DEAD SEA

MAIN NATURE PRESERVES

N

Elat Coral Beach Preserve

RED SEA

0   25 mi

50 km

◀ *The En Gedi Nature Preserve is a desert oasis near the Dead Sea. Waterfalls and streams produce lush vegetation, which attracts the leopard, the ibex, and the hyrax (rock-rabbit).*

a nonpolitical organization involved in programs to clean up beaches and the water. Water polluted by the intensive use of chemical fertilizers and pesticides has become a critical problem. One high priority is to treat waste water so that it can be used for irrigation purposes. Pollutant emissions caused by increased traffic are being combated by introducing cheaper lead-free gasoline. Other measures include the government's stipulation in 1995 that diesel fuel should contain no more than 0.2% sulfur — down from 0.3%.

KEY FACTS

● Wherever schoolchildren plant trees, they return every year to record the development of their saplings.
● Some forests are named after famous people, such as Queen Elizabeth II and President John F. Kennedy.
● Israel's worst forest fire occurred on July 2, 1995, near Jerusalem. About 2 million trees were destroyed.
● 60% of Elat's fresh water requirements are provided by desalination, a process of extracting salt from sea and brackish water.

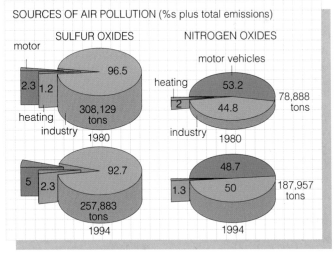

SOURCES OF AIR POLLUTION (%s plus total emissions)

SULFUR OXIDES — motor 2.3, 1.2, 96.5, heating, industry, 308,129 tons, 1980

NITROGEN OXIDES — motor vehicles 53.2, heating 2, 44.8, industry, 78,888 tons, 1980

SULFUR OXIDES — 5, 2.3, 92.7, 257,883 tons, 1994

NITROGEN OXIDES — 48.7, 1.3, 50, 187,957 tons, 1994

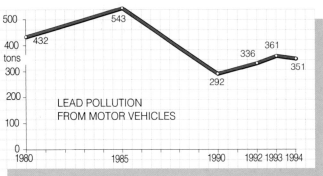

LEAD POLLUTION FROM MOTOR VEHICLES

500, 543
400, 432, tons
336, 361
300, 292, 351
200
100
0
1980   1985   1990   1992 1993 1994

Peace is vital for Israel and its neighbors. Since 1948, they have fought five wars. The hostility is rooted in the strong and ancient claims of two peoples to a small area of land. An acceptable solution to the Arab–Israeli conflict has yet to be agreed upon. Meanwhile, the cost in human life is high, and taxes, to pay for defense, are a heavy burden.

Egypt was the first Arab country to sign a peace treaty with Israel. As a result, in 1979 Prime Minister Begin of Israel and President Sadat of Egypt were jointly awarded the Nobel Peace Prize. Sadat was assassinated in 1981. In July 1994, King Hussein of Jordan and Prime Minister Rabin of Israel signed a peace accord. Almost a year later, Yitzhak Rabin was assassinated by a right-wing Jewish student. Many world leaders attended his funeral, including King Hussein.

In 1994, a new round of Middle East peace talks began. These are diplomatic discussions aimed at reaching agreement between Israel, Palestine, and all the neighboring Arab states. Cooperation and commitment are an important aspect of peace. Joint projects with Jordan and Egypt, such as sharing water and energy resources, are being planned within the framework of the peace talks. The creation of a Mediterranean and Middle East electricity grid, for example, would benefit a population of some 300 million people.

Many moderate Arabs and Jews support the peace process, because of its advantages for everyone in the Middle East. But the influence of religious and nationalist extremists on both sides has to be curtailed if the peace process is to succeed.

◀ *On November 4, 1995, Prime Minister Yitzhak Rabin was assassinated at a peace rally in Jerusalem. World leaders and old enemies came to Israel to pay their respects at his funeral.*

▼ *On September 4, 1996, Prime Minister Benjamin Netanyahu and Yasir Arafat, the leader of the PNA, met for the first time, to discuss the peace apparatus and to restore confidence in the peace process.*

KEY FACTS

● Israel's national anthem is called "Hatikva," which means "The Hope."
● In 1996, the first-ever scheduled El Al flight from Ben-Gurion Airport to Amman, the capital of Jordan, took place.
● There are a number of government initiatives for Israeli–Arab understanding. Givat Haviva and Neve Shalom/Wahat al-Salam are 2 institutions that teach peaceful coexistence to both adults and children.

FURTHER INFORMATION

●EMBASSY OF ISRAEL
3514 International Drive, N.W.
Washington, D. C. 20008
Provides information on Israel.
●AMERICAN ISRAEL PUBLIC AFFAIRS COMMITTEE
440 First Street, N.W.
Washington, D.C. 20001
●El Al Airlines
120 West 45 Street
New York, NY 10036
●ISRAEL GOVERNMENT TOURIST OFFICE
800 Second Avenue
New York, NY 10017
Provides information such as maps and pamphlets.
●KIBBUTZ REPRESENTATIVES
110 E. 59 Street
New York, NY 10022
Provides an information pack on kibbutzim.

BOOKS ABOUT ISRAEL
Gates, Fay C. *Judaism*. Facts on File, 1990

Odijk, Pamela. *Israelites*. Silver Burdett, 1990.

Penny, Sue. *Judaism* (Discovering Religions). Raintree Steck-Vaughn, 1997.

Pirotta, Saviour. *Jerusalem*. Silver Burdett, 1993.

Rogoff, Mike. *Israel*. (World in View). Raintree Steck-Vaughn, 1991.

GLOSSARY

ASHKENAZI
A term used to describe Jewish people from Central and Eastern Europe.

BAR MITZVAH or BAT MITZVAH
The religious celebration held for a Jewish boy or girl at the age of 13 when, according to tradition, he or she becomes an adult.

BEDOUIN
A tribal people who live in the Negev and Galilee. They make up 10% of Israel's Muslim Arab population. Only 40% still live a wholly nomadic life.

CHALLAH (plural CHALOT)
The Hebrew word for a braided loaf of bread. Two are eaten during the Sabbath meal.

COOPERATIVE
An association of farmers or other groups who pool their resources, work together, and share the profits.

DRUZE
A group of people whose religion contains elements of the Muslim faith, but with significant variations. About 95,000 live in northern Israel.

GROSS NATIONAL PRODUCT
The total value of all the goods and services produced by a country in a year.

HAGGADAH
The Haggadah tells the story of the exodus of the Israelites from Egypt more than 3,000 years ago. It is read on the first night of the Passover festival.

HAMANTASCHEN
A three-cornered pastry with a sweet poppy seed or prune filling that is eaten during the festival of Purim.

HOLOCAUST
The murder of six million Jews during World War II by the Nazi regime in Germany.

KIBBUTZ (plural KIBBUTZIM)
A cooperative farming community where people share ideals, responsibilities, and work. Instead of wages, the kibbutz provides its members with housing, education, and food.

KOSHER
Jewish dietary laws. They forbid the eating of all products derived from pigs and of shellfish, and stipulate that meat and dairy products should not be prepared or eaten together.

LATKE
A fried potato pancake eaten during the Hanukkah holiday.

MATZAH
Flat, unleavened bread (made without yeast), eaten during the Passover holiday.

MOSHAV (plural MOSHAVIM)
A farming community that is similar to a kibbutz, except that its members lead independent lives.

ORTHODOX JEW
Someone who keeps strictly to Jewish religious laws.

OTTOMAN TURKS
A Muslim people from Asia who conquered parts of southeast Europe, North Africa, and the Middle East around 1520. They later lost part of this territory, but remained in control of the Middle East till 1917.

SEPHARDI
A term used to describe Jewish people from North Africa, the Mediterranean area, and Arabic-speaking countries.

SHARAV
A hot, desert wind that blows from the southeast from May to mid-June and from September to October, filling the air with particles of sand. The Arabic name is "Khamsin."

SHERUT TAXI
A shared taxi that holds seven passengers and operates between two fixed points.

TERRACING
Cutting strips of farmland into the side of a hill, forming a pattern of "steps" in the hillside.

TORAH
A scroll containing the first five books of the Hebrew Bible.

ULTRA-ORTHODOX JEW
Someone who keeps strictly to Jewish religious laws, and also dresses in distinctive clothes. Men often study full-time in a religious center.

WADI
A dry riverbed in the desert that may suddenly fill with water after a rainstorm.

WEST BANK
The area west of the Jordan River and the Dead Sea controlled by Israel after the 1967 war. Control of much of the area passed to the Palestinian National Authority in 1995.

ZIONISM
The Zionist movement was formed in the late 19th century to campaign for a Jewish homeland in the Middle Eastern area where the Israelites had originally lived. "Zion" is another name for Jerusalem.

INDEX

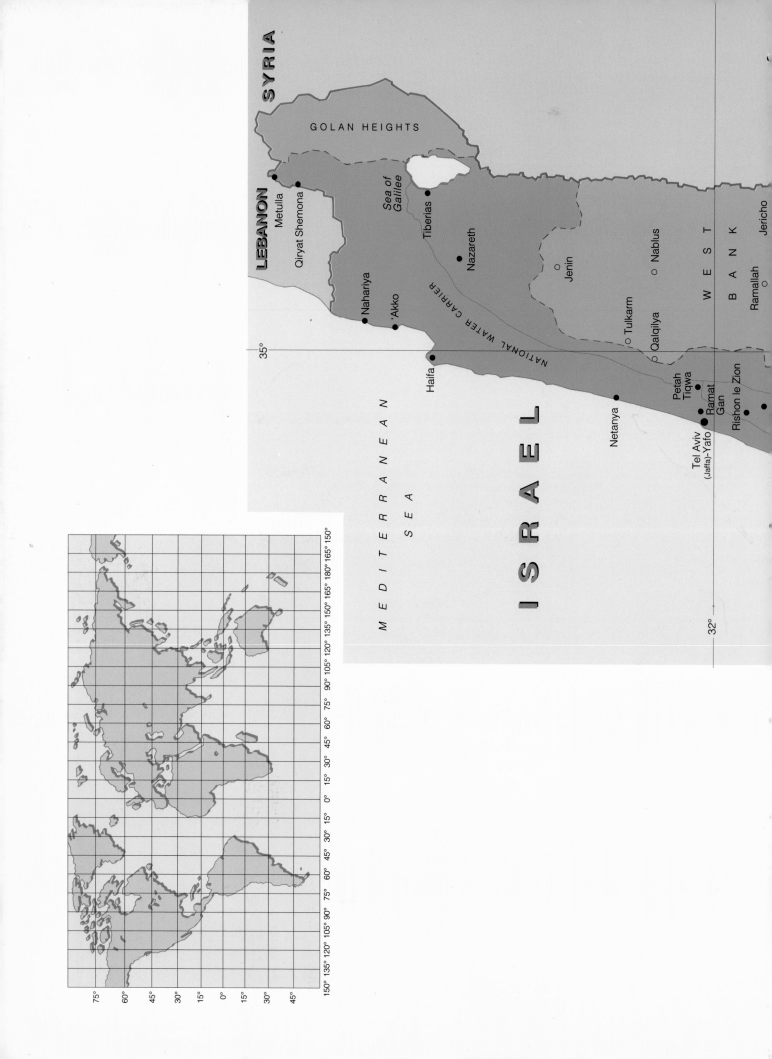

SYRIA

GOLAN HEIGHTS

LEBANON

Metulla

Qiryat Shemona

Sea of Galilee

Tiberias

Nazareth

Nahariya

'Akko

Jenin

Nablus

Tulkarm

Qalqilya

W   E   S   T

B   A   N   K

Ramallah

Jericho

Haifa

35°

NATIONAL WATER CARRIER

M E D I T E R R A N E A N

S E A

Netanya

Petah Tiqwa

Ramat Gan

Rishon le Zion

Tel Aviv (Jaffa)-Yafo

I S R A E L

32°

75°

60°

45°

30°

15°

0°

15°

30°

45°

150° 135° 120° 105° 90° 75° 60° 45° 30° 15° 0° 15° 30° 45° 60° 75° 90° 105° 120° 135° 150° 165° 180° 165° 150°

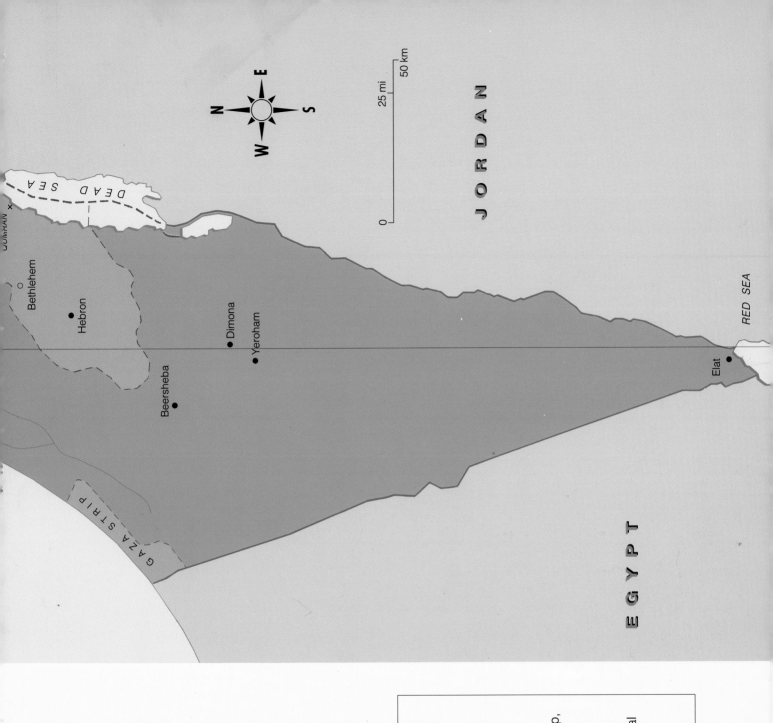